$\mathcal{T}$he reproduction of this old lantern slide shows Walter Beatty, a highly popular horse wrangler among Zion National Park visitors for years, introducing a guest to the beauties of the canyon from Observation Point on the East Rim.

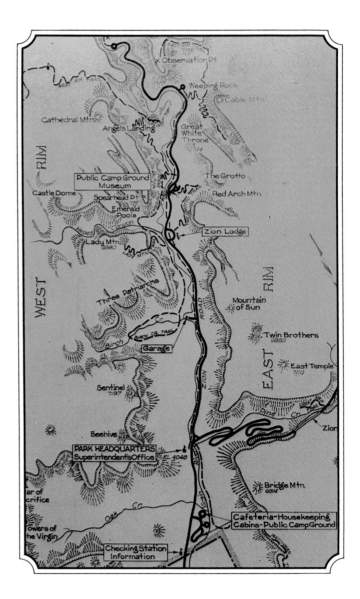

Zion Album

A Nostalgic History of Zion Canyon

By

J. L. Crawford

Published by the Zion Natural History Association,
Zion National Park, Springdale, Utah 84767

The author recognizes the contribution of Dr. Wesley Larsen who played a key role in retrieving the archived slides reproduced in this book.

ISBN: 0-915630-21-4

Library of Congress Catalog Card Number 85-51614

EDITORS   Victor L. Jackson
           David G. Ellingson

COVER DESIGN   Riddell Advertising & Design
DESIGNER/ILLUSTRATOR   Madaline Merry
Printed by Paragon Press

Zion Natural History Association
Zion National Park
Springdale, UT 84767
800-635-3959
E-mail: znha@infowest.com

To Stephen T. Mather,
father of our national parks,
and his assistant, Horace M. Albright,
patron saint of Zion.

Stephen T. Mather

Horace M. Albright

I wish to express my appreciation to the following persons for their efforts and contributions in making this book a success: Victor L. Jackson, Chief Park Naturalist, for recognizing the historical and artistic value of these hand-colored "lantern slides" and for conceiving the idea for this book as a means of preservation and presentation to the public; to Lindy Merry and Dave Ellingson for design, production and editing; to Bob Wood for his assistance in locating and photographing the old projector; to Margaret Malm, Kodak Laboratory technician and part-time VIP (Volunteer in Parks), for her work in copying the originals onto 35mm slides; to my wife, Fern, for her constructive criticism and patience; and to the board members of the Zion Natural History Association for their support of the project.

Contents

Introduction

Here is presented a representative selection of some priceless mementoes of Zion National Park's past. They are reproductions of the "lantern slides" that were used in the park naturalists' illustrated talks before the advent of color photography. There's quite a story behind the slides and this book, and I guess you could say my part in it began on January 5, 1914.

I was brought into the world by a midwife in a lumber shack about two hundred yards south of the present Zion Canyon Visitor Center. My first recollections are of green fields and orchards where the park's residential areas and campgrounds are now situated, irrigation ditches to keep it all green, and a clear brook coming out of Oak Creek Canyon. There were also some rather shabby farm buildings scattered throughout.

I was ten years old when the first graded road came to the canyon, and twenty before the road had anything better than a gravel surface. Like the road, living conditions were somewhat primitive for the first few years. We acquired running water in 1926 and electricity a year later. Transportation was by buggy, wagon or horseback until I was nine or ten, when some of my uncles began sporting Model T Fords. However, automobiles had ceased to be novelties a few

*I*n the early 1900s, my father built his farm just about where today's Zion Canyon Visitor Center stands in the park.

xi

years previously as the world began hearing about Zion National Park.

My brother Lloyd and I were both fascinated by automobiles. Lloyd, two years older than I, wasn't afflicted by my chronic bashfulness, and I became his shadow. If a car stopped in our neighborhood, he would be right there looking it over while I stood back a little. With the help of pictures in magazines, we became experts at identifying the cars that came into the park—the Jewett, Moon, Star, Overland, Willys Knight and many more, including the rare and expensive Rickenbacker, Deusenberg and Cunningham. And who could forget the air-cooled Franklin? (Lloyd, by the way, became an outstanding auto mechanic.)

My father was a farmer and a some-

My parents honeymooned in their wagon far up Zion Canyon. Note the string my father used to trip the shutter for this "self-portrait." Years later, I earned money from my garden in the canyon. Surrounding me are brother Lloyd, sister Elva, and baby LaDessa.

---

times photographer, so we had farm produce and postcard pictures of the canyon to sell to the tourists we could stop with our crude signs. I was encouraged to grow a garden of my own, and was allowed to keep the income from it. My most profitable crop was cantaloupes. Through the sale of these commodities, we made friends with many campers and a few artists and photographers. Probably the most famous painter we knew was Gunnar Widforss, the "painter of the Grand Canyon." I became better acquainted with him when I worked at the North Rim in 1932.

I was eleven years old when Angus M. Woodbury became Zion National Park's first naturalist. He held the position from 1925 to 1933, being present in the park only during the summer months; he was a member of the Dixie Junior College faculty in St. George, Utah, and later transferred to the University of Utah in Salt Lake City.

Woodbury's work in Zion was significant, even though Lloyd and I made pests of ourselves following him around as he collected reptiles, insects and plants for exhibits and scientific collections. We, of course, made our contributions, especially when we found strange-looking beetles. Woodbury's

*T*he huge old projector now rests among the park's artifacts.

interests covered all phases of the Zion story. Besides gathering data, he wrote and published scientific papers and started a library. He was an authority on the biota and history of the area, and he possessed a reasonable knowledge of geology.

Nature walks and campfire programs were some of the services Woodbury and other staff members provided the park visitor from the beginning, and within three years a small museum was opened. Talks by ranger-naturalists became a regular part of the evening programs at Zion Lodge, not far up the canyon from my parents' home.

Later, when I became a dishwasher at the lodge, I would stand by a window of the recreation hall and listen to the park naturalists as they told the Zion story with the aid of colored slides—that is, if I got the dishes washed in time. The lantern-slide projector the naturalists used was enormous, measuring at least two feet in length. The speaker signaled for a change of slide with the tap of

a cane on the floor, the flash of a small flashlight, or a snapping toy such as came in Cracker Jacks.

Much time and effort was required to accumulate a sufficient number of slides on the various subjects. The slides consisted of a positive print on glass, hand-colored and protected by a piece of clear glass of the same size bound to it with adhesive tape. A black paper mask provided a border. The finished product was a color transparency "floated" in glass measuring 3¼ x 4 inches.

The coloring must have been very tedious and exacting work, but most of the slides look very professional, despite some deterioration on several. Very few carry the identification of the photographer or processor, but it is known that the Zion Picture Shop, owned and operated by Randall Jones and his son Homer in Cedar City, Utah, supplied many of them. They did both the photography and hand-coloring. The finish work was often done by companies as far away as New York, Chicago and Los Angeles.

*M*y work as a ranger took me all over Zion's backcountry in the '50s.

---

it must have been the ranger-naturalists' evening talks that influenced my choice of studies and career aims.

I attended elementary school in Springdale and high school at Hurricane, twenty-five miles west, where I lived with relatives as there were no school buses at that time. Getting through college was difficult, and took me fourteen years, beginning at Dixie College in St. George and ending with a B.S. degree at Brigham Young University in 1947. The period July, 1941, through September, 1945, was spent in the armed forces.

After World War II, I worked for two summers as a seasonal naturalist at Zion National Park and Cedar Breaks National Monument as I completed my university studies during the winters. In January, 1948, I received my appointment as a park ranger, serving at Zion and Bryce Canyon until November, 1953, when I resigned in deference to the position that my wife Fern held as the mainstay in the family's mercantile business.

Perhaps much of the actual photography was done by the park staff, including Woodbury, Superintendent E. T. Scoyen, Rangers Arden Schiefer and Harold Russell, and later, Clifford C. Presnall, who replaced Woodbury as chief park naturalist in 1933. Whoever did the work, I always enjoyed seeing the slides projected at the lodge. I suppose, too, that I was always fascinated by the Park Service uniform, but

xv

I built a small motel in Panguitch, Utah, but because of the seasonal nature of that business, I accepted a position as county welfare director. I kept it for thirteen years, managing the motel in the evenings. When the state of Utah abolished the county welfare departments and adopted a regional system, I looked again to the National Park Service, where I found I still had many friends. I returned to Zion as a ranger.

Soon afterward, I accepted the position as assistant chief park naturalist, we disposed of the motel, Fern turned her job over to her brother and his boys, and we spent seven pleasant years in Zion Canyon. In 1980, I retired and we moved to our new home in St. George.

Even before the time I was at the park, those glass lantern slides had been largely forgotten. They were stored away when color photography and smaller film slides came into general use about the time of World War II.

The old slides were recently "discovered," and their quality and historical value recognized. Much thought was given to a possible means of presenting them to the public. This book is the result.

In deciding on a format, the first thought was to reproduce the naturalists' talks as presented on the various subjects. There was just one obstacle. It seems there was never one talk written or recorded. At least none has been found. So it fell to me — the one park employee who grew up in the area and was old enough to know, personally, most of those pioneer naturalists and rangers — to select the pictures to be used here, separate them into categories and provide captions. This work came about during my continuing involvement with the Zion Natural History Association and it helps maintain my status as a Volunteer in Parks (VIP), doing occasional work on Zion's historic photo file.

So this book is a subjective, nostalgic history of Zion. What you see is the best of the applicable slides on the subjects of pre-history, exploration and settlement of Zion Canyon and the immediate area, and the development of Zion National Park, with appropriate narrative. The book is not a comprehensive chronology, a geology text, nor a checklist of plants and animals. Information on all of those subjects is readily available from the staff and other publications at the park's visitor centers in Zion Canyon and the Kolob Canyons Section. It is my intention that, in looking over these hand-painted relics of the early days of Zion, you will get the story, in brief, almost like those first naturalists told it.

J.L. Crawford

Prehistory

To the pioneers who settled in and near Zion Canyon in the 1860s, the mysterious people who had built the mud and stone structures that still remain in a few of the alcoves were "Cliff Dwellers." To the first naturalists of Zion National Park, these American Indians were "Basket Makers" and "Pueblos." The now common term "Anasazi" was not yet in their vocabulary, although archaeologist A. V. Kidder suggested the name for the combined Basket Maker-Pueblo sequence in 1927.

This culture centered about the Four Corners area, where the present borders of Utah, Arizona, New Mexico and Colorado meet. It flourished from about 45 A.D. to the late Thirteenth Century, when a series of droughts brought about its decline. By 1500, the arrival of Athabascan tribes (Navajo and Apache) from the north caused the final abandonment of the region by the Anasazi.

Zion Canyon, being situated on the periphery of the Anasazi region, cannot boast the elaborate pueblos or villages that have been left nearer the Four Corners. Perhaps the Zion residents were the poor country cousins of the Mesa Verde "city dwellers," or maybe this area had been vacated by the time the Pueblo culture reached its peak. Certainly the area was a

*A*nasazi ruins in the park were the subject of archaeological digs—and horseback tours—in the 1930s. Private lands limit access today.

frontier of sorts, and it may have been pressured by enemies from the west and north.

A frontier it remained as the Anasazi were replaced by Athabascan stock south of the Colorado River and the linguistically unrelated Shoshonean tribes on the north, such as the Utes and Paiutes. Various Paiute sub-tribes occupied the country surrounding Zion Canyon. They were rendered destitute by the depredations of the warlike Navajos from beyond the Colorado. Those who lived in the immediate vicinity of Zion called themselves Parrusits and the river along which they lived Pah-roos. Although they hunted the canyon in groups, and in daylight, they would not go in alone nor remain after dark. This was due to the presence of two deities, Kai-ne-sava and Wai-no-pits, whom they feared or respected, wrote Angus Woodbury in *A History of Southern Utah and Its National Parks*.

The nomadic Paiutes lived mainly in temporary structures made from branches and plants. The few stone and mud structures still standing in the park are of Anasazi origin, and they are small, being storage bins rather than dwellings. Most are located in a section of the park that is difficult for the public to reach due to the necessity of crossing private land. Zion is not an archaeological area, but rather a geologic gem in which Triassic and Jurassic layers are beautifully exhibited. To those interested in the ancient residents of the region, we recommend the several national parks and monuments throughout the Four Corners area in which the Anasazi story is magnificently told.

*N*o one has yet found the key to translating the Anasazi petroglyphs found in and around Zion Canyon.

*A*ncient inscriptions in the park may be called "petroglyphs" or "pictographs" interchangeably. But the first term has come to identify that which is incised or carved, while the latter refers to painted figures. Some pictographs still have bright red or green pigments, which may be at least 1,500 years old.

*B*y choosing a patch of the dark, mineral stain called
"desert varnish" for a canvas, the artist accomplished two
objectives: contrast and permanence. The Anasazi
lived with nature and probably hunted the bighorn sheep
depicted, competing with wolves and other predators.

_W_ai-no-pits was the devil spirit who kept the Parrusits out of the canyon after sundown. The earlier Anasazi must not have known about him, as they built this small granary far up the canyon, near Weeping Rock. They also built a trail up the canyon wall nearby, the carved steps of which are visible at one point along the East Rim Trail.

hief Ranger Donal J. Jolley, who worked at the park from 1920 to 1943, inspects ancient Anasazi structures that are obviously food storage bins. Many kinds of wild seeds were gathered and stored. Domestic crops such as corn and squash—and perhaps beans—were cultivated. The bins' openings were probably sealed with mud and rocks against rodents.

hese were called "cliff dwellings" until someone discovered that they were too small for human habitation. But what was the collapsed portion like? It may have been a residence.

*O*utlines of several pueblos have been excavated on the valley floor near the confluence of the two branches of the Virgin River, but no dwellings have been found standing.

Exploration and Settlement

Considering the number of explorers and trappers who traversed the Zion area, it is surprising that none of them entered the canyon prior to the arrival of a Mormon scout in 1858. However, there were several "near misses," beginning 82 years earlier when the Dominguez-Escalante party, named after the two Spanish priests leading it, crossed the Virgin River twenty miles to the west.

Their objective was to establish a northern route between Santa Fe, New Mexico, and Monterey, California. They abandoned the plan at about the halfway point, the leaders deciding to return to Santa Fe by a more southerly route. On October 14, 1776, they camped near the present site of Toquerville, Utah, and the next day crossed the Virgin River just below the thermal spring between present-day La Verkin and Hurricane. Because of the spring's odor, they applied the name "Rio Sulfúreo" to the river. The expedition diary indicates that they saw the cliffs of Zion from near that point.

Father Escalante had dreams of establishing missions and presidios along their route, but his plans never materialized. It was fifty years before the next European ventured into the area.

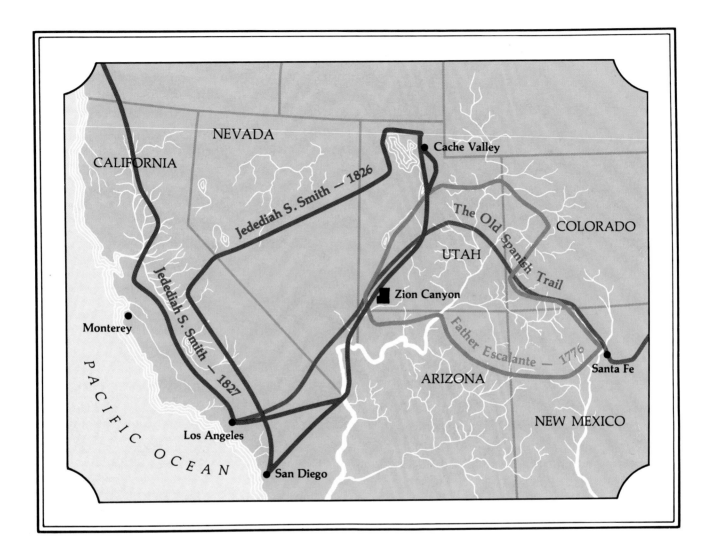

$\mathcal{M}$ajor explorers of the Zion area were Father Escalante (gold route), Jedediah Strong Smith (red), and others who followed the Old Spanish Trail (brown).

Father Escalante

This was the "Gentleman Trapper," Jedediah Strong Smith, a paragon among Western mountain men. Second to none but Lewis and Clark as an explorer of the West, Smith was the first to reach California from the American frontier, first to cross the Sierras, first to traverse the Great Basin in two directions, and first to reach Oregon up the California coast. In ten years, he saw more of the West than any other man of his time.

Yet Smith's purpose was not to explore, but to pursue his business as a fur trapper and trader. He made two trips from northern Utah to California in 1826 and 1827. On the 1826 journey, he followed the Virgin River from Escalante's crossing down to its confluence with the Colorado. Smith named the stream the "Adams River" in honor of President John Quincy Adams. Emerging from the rugged Virgin River Gorge, Smith followed that section of the river from near the present site of Littlefield, Arizona, to St. Thomas, Nevada, which later became part of the Old Spanish Trail. (St. Thomas now lies under the waters behind Hoover Dam.)

Others followed Jedediah Smith's trailblazing. When Antonio Armijo led a trading expedition to California in 1829-1830, he back-tracked Escalante's route into southwestern Utah, where he picked up Smith's trail. Also in 1829, Ewing Young, with a company of fur trappers, traveled from Taos, New Mexico, to California by turning onto Smith's trail in central Utah.

William Wolfskill made a similar trip in 1830, but deviated just north of the Zion area to trap to the headwaters of the Sevier River, which he named in honor of General John Sevier of Kentucky. Wolfskill continued trapping along the Virgin and Colorado Rivers before arriving in California, where he remained.

Between the time of the Wolfskill expedition and the U.S.-Mexican signing of the Treaty of Guadelupe Hidalgo in 1848, the Old Spanish Trail became the Spaniards' regular highway between the missions in New Mexico and California. Though the Spaniards established only part of the trail, it was during this time that Spanish names were applied to several features in this vicinity, such as Santa Clara Creek, La Verkin (La Virgen) Creek, the Virgin River (Rio Virgen), and Las Vegas (The Meadows).

Some historians believe the names of

William Wolfskill

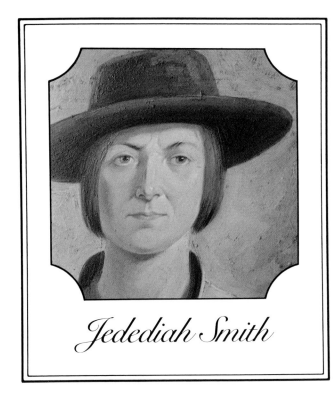

Jedediah Smith

both the Virgin and Sevier Rivers were applied by the Spaniards and have since been switched through errors on maps. The placid nature of the Sevier lends credence to the supposition, and it is true that Armijo called the turbulent Virgin "Rio Severo" in 1830. There is no documented evidence that the Sevier was ever called the Virgin, however.

The Virgin was called "the most dreary river I have ever seen" by Captain John C. Fremont in 1844. He saw the stream not where it dashes over the rocks in Zion, but where it oozes onto the barren Mojave Desert. Fremont was on his way from California, following the route blazed by Jedediah Smith, Wolfskill and others. Fremont's account of his expedition was used by the Mormons who settled Utah on their exodus from the Midwest. (Years later, Mormons at Parowan, Utah, not far north of Zion, rescued Fremont from winter exposure and starvation while he was on another journey.)

John Fremont

Soon after Brigham Young led the Mormons into Salt Lake Valley in 1847, the Old Spanish Trail was destined to become the Mormon Trail. Late that year, Captain Jefferson Hunt led a Mormon party to California for the purpose of purchasing seed and farm animals. Returning members of the Mormon Battalion brought the first wagon over the trail, and it soon became the regular thoroughfare for California-bound gold-seekers and immigrants.

Part of one group which Hunt led in 1849, not trusting his leadership, broke off and took a more westerly route than the Mormon Trail. They perished in the desert, giving Death Valley its name.

It was another Mormon scout who "discovered" Zion Canyon in 1858. By then, Brigham Young had established his Iron and Cotton Missions in southern Utah. Part of

Young's strategy in working toward Mormon self-sufficiency and independence was to colonize as much of the area as possible, taking advantage of available resources such as soil, water and minerals. The Iron Mission resulted from the discovery of iron ore and coal near the present site of Cedar City. A little farther south, the Cotton Mission was established on the Virgin River, where the climate was conducive to the growing of that fiber crop as well as many kinds of fruit.

14

Several towns were soon to be found in Utah's "Dixie." Among their inhabitants was young Nephi Johnson, a missionary to the Paiute Indians and an interpreter for emigrant parties. On Young's orders, Johnson explored the upper Virgin River Valley, going from Toquerville with a Paiute guide. Because of the Paiute superstition about the devil spirit Wai-no-pits, the guide refused to go beyond the present site of the park's Zion Canyon Visitor Center. Johnson is thought to have penetrated the canyon as far as The Narrows. His recommendations led to the establishment of settlements in and near Zion Canyon as part of the Cotton Mission.

Nephi Johnson

16

*C*amps like this were a familiar scene as settlement spread in all directions from the center of the Cotton Mission. Sometimes the covered wagon boxes were lifted off the wheels and set on the ground for "houses." The camps were often bases for builders of the roads and irrigation ditches necessary to the survival of the new, small communities. In December, 1858, Nephi Johnson supervised the building of a passable road up the Hurricane Fault. This section of primitive road, now part of the paved approach to Zion, was appropriately called the "Johnson Twist."

*A*lthough most of those called by Brigham Young to the Dixie Cotton Mission responded willingly, they found the existence difficult and lonely. The wistful message carved in small letters beside the stylized cotton-plant "petroglyph" says: "Jacob Peart Jr I was set her to rais cotton march 1858." It's still visible, carved in a cliff on the west side of Interstate 15, just south of St. George. The larger letters are latter-day graffiti.

17

*B*y 1862, there were ten settlements between the Johnson Twist and Zion Canyon, several soon to be abandoned due to the rampages of the Virgin River. Grafton was the first casualty. Washed from the sandy site in this photo, Grafton was relocated on higher ground a mile up the river. But it became a ghost town by 1940.

*T*he abandoned Oliver DeMille rock house is testament to a measure of luxury enjoyed by at least one family for a few years at Shunesburg. Residents of other towns traveled many miles to attend parties and dances in this house. Devastating floods during the 1890s sealed the fate of Shunesburg, but in the mid-1980s a new owner began planning the house's restoration.

18

In 1862, several families settled near some large springs in Zion Canyon and called the place Springdale. When they began experiencing chills and fever, they moved to higher ground. It is one of three "upriver" towns to survive, along with Rockville and Virgin. The foreground in this picture, a downriver view to the south and west, became part of Zion National Park in the land purchase of 1931.

A crude road was built into the canyon where the settlers gathered firewood and pastured their animals. Isaac Behunin, who named Zion Canyon, built a cabin and farmed the land near the present site of Zion Lodge. A few other families joined his, but none remained more than a few years.

*S*mall farms and orchards extended up Zion Canyon almost to the end of the present road at the Temple of Sinawava. Although the road stopped two miles short of that point until 1924, it was visited frequently, the river and its flood plain serving as a reasonable wagon road.

*I*n 1888, fifteen-year-old David Flanigan conceived the idea of a "wire" to carry lumber from the plateau to the canyon floor. The Zion Cable became a reality thirteen years later, and is described in the book *The Outstanding Wonder*, available at the park's visitor centers. The draw works in the foreground of this picture were located on the riverbank near Weeping Rock, below Cable Mountain.

*D*iminishing farmlands in the upper Virgin River towns brought about the birth of two new communities, Hurricane and La Verkin, soon after the turn of the century. Canals carrying river water to each town were ambitious undertakings, providing irrigation for hundreds of fertile acres which were safe from the flooding river.

21

Naming the Peaks

W ho gave Zion Canyon's peaks their names? The question can be answered only in part. A few names can be traced to definite persons or events, but some, like Topsy, just grew.

One would suppose the Mormons who first occupied the canyon bestowed those names which carry religious connotations, but such is not the case. My father, William Louis Crawford, began photographing the area around the turn of the century. Not many of his surviving pictures have titles, and those that have don't show much originality. A view of Mt. Kinesava from Rockville is called "North Mountain," while The Sentinel, viewed from Oak Creek, is also called "North Mountain." "Pine Creek Peaks" included The East Temple; "Birch Creek Peaks" included the Altar of Sacrifice.

Clarence Dutton, of the United States Geological Survey, referred to the Western and Eastern Temples and Towers of the Virgin in his 1882 report, but the locals knew nothing of that report, so the West Temple remained "Steamboat Mountain" to them—as it still does to some.

Frederick Vining Fisher, a Methodist minister from Ogden, Utah, visited Zion in September, 1916, and was accompanied up

*F*rederick Vining Fisher, who named many of Zion's peaks, said "never have I seen such a sight before" when he viewed this scene in the late afternoon sun. According to Angus Woodbury, Fisher added that "it is by all odds America's masterpiece. . . . I have looked for this mountain all my life but I never expected to find it in this world. This is The Great White Throne."

the canyon by Claud Hirschi—a Mormon youth from Rockville—and a friend by the name of Bingham. The trio decided to name the points as they rode along. It isn't known what happened to their list nor how many of the names were rejected, but Angus Woodbury attributes the Three Patriarchs, The Great White Throne and The Great Organ (now The Organ) to this party. H. L. Reid credits the naming of Angels Landing to Fisher as well. It is quite possible that The Watchman, The Sentinel and Altar of Sacrifice were also named that day, although there is no record remaining to document that notion.

Certainly credit for many of the names, especially of less prominent features and backcountry place names, should go to Richard T. Evans, who made the topographical survey of the park during the 1920s and 1930s, and to Herbert E. Gregory, pioneer geologist, who wrote USGS Paper 220. Gregory's paper was the "bible" of Zion geology for many years.

Johnson Mountain was named for Mormon scout Nephi Johnson, the "discoverer" of Zion Canyon. It is a southward extension of The Watchman and looks down on Shunesburg, now a ghost town.

The Watchman was Flanigan's Peak to early residents of Springdale, who identified it with the family that farmed at its base. It was renamed The Watchman by virtue of its imposing position guarding the entrance to Zion Canyon.

*B*ridge Mountain gets its name from a natural arch on its face—the "flying buttress" shown below. The arch may be viewed from the Zion Canyon Visitor Center. To residents in the late 1800s, this was Crawford Mountain, because my grandfather's farm touched the lower slopes.

Clarence Dutton wrote about the two "temples" on opposite sides of the valley, so the taller, more massive one became The West Temple. It remains Steamboat Mountain to the old-timers. The East Temple is viewed here from a gallery where cars used to be allowed to stop in the Zion-Mount Carmel Tunnel.

*M*ount Spry was named for William Spry, the governor of Utah from 1908 to 1916 and a major influence in the creation of Zion National Park. The peak is flanked by The East Temple on the right, the Twin Brothers and the Mountain of the Sun on the left.

*T*he Altar of Sacrifice, one of the Towers of the Virgin, is white sandstone streaked with red from the heavily pigmented remnant of Temple Cap formation above.

28

*W*hen a trio of pinnacles came into the view of Reverend Frederick Vining Fisher, sixteen-year-old Claud Hirschi said "Abraham, Isaac and Jacob." According to Angus Woodbury's account, the Methodist minister agreed with his guide that the peaks should be the Three Patriarchs. The peak called Jacob is nearly masked in this view by the redder Mount Moroni, which is closer to the foreground.

*W*hen Fisher noticed that Hirschi and his friend had stopped, he asked them why. One replied that they were "waiting for the organist to come and play The Great Organ," Woodbury writes. The Organ, as it is now called, appears to the right of The Great White Throne when viewed from the upcanyon side.

*A*ngels Landing is opposite the Great White Throne and not nearly as tall or imposing. Reverend Fisher, says H. Lorenzo Reid's *Dixie of the Desert*, felt that "the Angels would never land on the Throne, but would reverently pause at the foot."

30

The Virgin River meanders past The Organ and Angels Landing, which are an extension of the greater mass of Mount Majestic.

*S*nowclad after a winter storm, The Spearhead serves as a facade for the taller Mount Majestic behind it. Angels Landing is to the right.

The Sentinel stands straight and tall beside The Beehives and The Streaked Wall. This mountain gave up a great part of its mass more than 3,500 years ago in a massive landslide that dammed the river and left the Sand Bench.

Red Arch Mountain looms above the Grotto Picnic Area. About 1880, a great mass of rock fell from the face, enlarging the arch. The rock covered a spring which O. D. Gifford, a Springdale resident, had been using to irrigate a field of corn. Gifford abandoned the site.

33

*V*iewed from Zion Lodge, this peak catches the first and last rays of the sun, so it was named Mountain of the Sun.

*T*he name Lady Mountain won over Mount Zion, which park officials preferred, because someone saw the likeness of a woman on the cliff.

$\mathcal{A}$ look at the Mountain of Mystery requires a one-mile walk to the end of the Gateway to The Narrows Trail.

Oak Creek Village

Crawford Peak hadn't been named at all when my grandfather started his farm at its base. In 1879, William Robinson Crawford moved from Rockville to Oak Creek, which flows past the present Zion Canyon Visitor Center in the park. There, he purchased a small parcel of land and homesteaded many acres more.

The task of building irrigation ditches for his farm, fences, a barn and a home was monumental, but once established, the farm provided the Crawfords a good living. Eleven children grew to maturity, and the family remained largely self-sufficient. There was a shop for everything—a blacksmith shop, a sheetmetal shop, a carpenter shop, a wagon assembly shed, even a shoe shop. An overshot waterwheel powered a turning lathe and a grist mill, too. The eldest son, John, later installed a hydraulic ram to lift water to his hilltop home.

After the property was divided among the six sons, extracting a living from the smaller parcels became increasingly difficult. Consider the changing economy, the aging of the sons and the reluctance of the third generation to remain on their small farms when wage-paying employment beckoned them.

$\mathscr{A}$ point high on Bridge Mountain affords a bird's-eye view of Oak Creek, that part of Springdale which bordered the south boundary of the park.

In 1931, after William R. Crawford had long since passed on, the federal government inquired about buying the property, which was adjacent to the park. The sons consented to sell, against the wishes of their aging mother. They all knew about the possibility of condemnation proceedings, and they agreed with the park officials that their village was an eyesore—only two homes had ever known paint.

Through the purchase, the government eliminated part of this "undesirable approach" to the park. And the park thereby obtained much-needed room for utility installations and residences for personnel. This move also placed within the park boundary one of the finest viewpoints in the canyon, as well as the future site of the present Zion Canyon Visitor Center and Administration Building.

What did the owners receive in payment for their property? Louis Crawford, my father, owned about 360 acres, including most of Oak Creek Canyon. The amount he was paid matched, almost to the dollar, the figure I paid forty years later for a lot in St. George, Utah, just large enough for one home. But that was 1931.

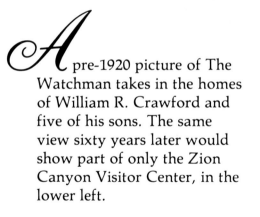

A pre-1920 picture of The Watchman takes in the homes of William R. Crawford and five of his sons. The same view sixty years later would show part of only the Zion Canyon Visitor Center, in the lower left.

*L*ouis Crawford's farm was the future site of the Zion Canyon Visitor Center. The vantage point for what had been called "the outstanding skyline in all the world" by a magazine writer certainly should be inside the park, the government reasoned. Also, the irrigation ditch (treeline on the hillside), along with several others, headed inside the park boundary.

*G*reen pastures and orchards provided a pleasing foreground for the majestic mountain backdrop, but a neglected field together with many shabby buildings added up to an "undesirable approach" the National Park Service wished to eliminate.

*C*rude footbridges afforded access to the "over-the-river" fields and outbuildings. Sometimes they were placed inside the park as access to diversion dams, flumes and the like.

*T*rees bordering ditch-banks would disappear with the elimination of the cultivated fields and irrigation ditches.

*F*rom Grandma Crawford's pea patch the foreground of
this view of The Watchman would soon change to include a
cafeteria, cabins and a campground.

Park
Establishment
and
Development

It is a generally accepted notion that the early Mormon settlers were blind to the beauties of Zion Canyon, their energies being directed to the task of extracting a livelihood from a hostile environment. Such was not the case. Although little has been recorded on the subject, it is known that the canyon was called "Joseph's Glory" for a time after Joseph Black, one of Springdale's first settlers, so enthusiastically extolled its beauties. It was the grandeur of "God's temples" that inspired Isaac Behunin to call the canyon "Little Zion." Also, Brigham Young, president of the Mormon Church, counselled discouraged residents of Springdale to stay, as someone would need to host the thousands who would eventually come to see the canyon.

It remained for John Wesley Powell, Clarence Dutton and Frederick S. Dellenbaugh, all of the United States Geological Survey—as well as Captain George Wheeler of the United States Army Corps of Engineers—to bring the scenic and scientific values of the canyon to the attention of the nation. Dellenbaugh called the canyon a "New Valley of Wonders" in his title for an article widely read in the January, 1904, issue of *Scribner's* magazine. Visitation to the area began to increase, and so did urgings that the canyon be protected as a special place.

*S*tephen T. Mather became the first director of the National Park Service in April, 1917. He first visited Zion in November, 1919, when Zion became a national park. Both events resulted from the tireless efforts of Mather's assistant, Horace M. Albright.

A proclamation creating Mukuntuweap National Monument, as Zion's first set-aside section was called, was signed by President Taft on July 31, 1909. The Assistant Secretary of the Interior had placed the proclamation on the President's desk about a month after receiving a report from the local United States surveyor, Leo A. Snow. Snow stated that "a view can be had of this canyon surpassed only by a similar view of the Grand Canyon of the Colorado . . . . In my opinion this canyon should be set apart by the government as a national park."

Horace M. Albright, assistant director of the National Park Service, visited Mukuntuweap several times as he worked to improve and enlarge the monument, bringing it to national-park status. He had been an assistant to the Secretary of the Interior, and had helped Stephen T. Mather formulate policy for administering the parks before the creation of the National Park Service in 1916. Mather was its first director, succeeded after his death by Albright.

Albright had often commended Zion residents for their attitude and cooperation in giving up grazing and farming privileges to help create a national park, as well as the inconvenience of equipping their wagons with wider, 4-inch tires that would not damage the roads or soil. The park was to mean improved roads for the residents, and a better way of life.

Frederick S. Dellenbaugh, at Zion Lodge in 1930, displays the flag that accompanied him and Major John Wesley Powell down the Grand Canyon in the boat *Emma Dean* during 1871 and 1872. Dellenbaugh's visit to Zion Canyon in 1903 and subsequent lectures and magazine articles probably had much to do with the canyon being designated a national monument in 1909.

*D*irector Mather became an enthusiastic champion of Zion, and visited the area several more times. This bronze tablet honoring him, designed by Bryant Baker, graces the entrance wall at the Zion Canyon Visitor Center.

*H*eber J. Grant, president of the Church of Jesus Christ of Latter-day Saints and a personal friend of Mather, journeyed from Salt Lake City to attend the dedication of the Mather plaque on July 4, 1932. Originally embedded in this rock on the Gateway to The Narrows Trail, the plaque was dislodged by a flash flood some twenty years later and was lost in the river sand. It was retrieved by Ted Whitmoyer, an enterprising seasonal naturalist, using a war-surplus metal detector.

*F*lash flooding also carried away the first bridge across the Virgin River. This one replaced it in 1924, built a little higher and more substantial than the first.
The Mountain of the Sun and the Twin Brothers tower above the bridge.

*R*oads and vehicles have changed since Zion became a national park, but The Watchman changes not in our lifetime.

*P*hotographed from Observation Point on the East Rim, this view reveals the newly completed road, built in 1923-1924. The first road to extend beyond the Grotto Campground (now the Grotto Picnic Area), it opened the canyon to travel as far as the Temple of Sinawava.

*T*he new road followed Big Bend past The Great Organ, the cable, and the Big Bend Trail. Just out of view are Raspberry Bend and Limekiln Point. All of these were local place names, and are no longer in use. The trail, for instance, is now the East Rim Trail. The road came too late to be helpful to users of the cable or kiln, but it served thousands of park visitors annually.

*T*he road ended at the Temple of Sinawava, one mile below the lower end of The Narrows. This is where park policy was relaxed in 1927, when a Hollywood movie company was permitted to build a replica of a Spanish hacienda for the filming of *Ramona*.

*O*ldest among the park's stone buildings is this one made of native, hammer-dressed sandstone. It houses a Park Service employee and his family at the Grotto Picnic Area, which until 1935 was the only campground in the park. This was the original Visitor Center, opening in 1928.

$\mathcal{Z}$ion Lodge, initially owned and operated by the Utah Parks Company, a subsidiary of the Union Pacific Railroad, began operation in 1925. It replaced the old Wylie Way Camp, a complex of wooden-floored tents set up by a Montana school teacher for early tourists.

*S*now creates a beautiful blanket on the canyon. Winters are mild and the park remains open all year. You may find the lodge closed in the winter, but accommodations are always available in nearby communities.

$\mathcal{U}$tility structures installed at the Court of the Patriarchs included a garage, a horse barn, a photo lab and a powerhouse. Commercial electricity didn't come to Zion until 1927.

$\mathcal{W}$ater storage tanks were unobtrusively placed below Red Arch Mountain.

*A*n attractive native stone entrance station was built by Civilian Conservation Corps labor. Several utility buildings, trails and fences were constructed by the Depression-born organization, which had two camps within the park during the early 1930s.

*T*he new South Campground Amphitheater was the site of Zion's first special Easter program in 1935, an annual pageant until 1941. The newly completed cafeteria, shown at the left, now serves as the Zion Nature Center.
(This is the only known photograph of the amphitheater site just after construction. The crack shows how the glass slides can be damaged—one reason we decided to print them.)

*N*aturalist-guided walks were instituted in the mid-1920s, as many miles of trails had been completed by then. The park's first naturalist, Angus M. Woodbury, uses his hat to point out features in The Stadium on the Gateway to The Narrows Trail. The Mather plaque is on the rock at right.

This party took to the East Rim Trail to view Lady Mountain, thus avoiding the great American disease Ranger-Naturalist H. L. Reid called "cushionitis."

*G*uided horseback trips were traditional at Zion beginning in the early 1920s. Walter Beatty, popular wrangler for the Utah Parks Company from about 1923 to 1950, is shown halting his party on the slickrock of the West Rim Trail to "breathe" the mounts.

*W*alters Wiggles, the switchbacks in the center of the photo, are easily negotiated by hikers and horses. The construction is named for Walter Ruesch, first custodian of Zion National Park, who supervised the building of the West Rim Trail in 1924. The half-mile spur from here to the summit of Angels Landing is strictly for hikers who do not suffer from acrophobia.

$\mathcal{A}$ magnificent view of Phantom Valley and the Great West Canyon rewards hikers or riders on the West Rim. Here, in the shade of ponderosa pines, members of horseback parties, as guests of the Utah Parks Company, could enjoy box lunches prepared by cooks at Zion Lodge.

*W*ith Angels Landing as a backdrop, tired riders—and horses—are on the home stretch from the 14-mile round trip to the West Rim.

60

By foot or horseback, a trip to either rim reveals the flatness of the Markagunt Plateau surrounding the canyon, such as the top of Deertrap Mountain.

One could opt for a ride through Echo Canyon to the East Rim and Observation Point, a somewhat shorter trip than the West Rim ride. Horseback trips on this trail have been discontinued, and the route is strictly for hikers.

$\mathcal{A}$ drive to the East Entrance, via the Zion-Mount Carmel Tunnel, begins by crossing Pine Creek on a beautiful sandstone arch bridge in which every color of rock found in the park is incorporated. Harry Langley, the landscape architect who designed the bridge, built a miniature model out of green laundry soap before the actual construction began in 1929.

$\mathcal{H}$ ighway switchbacks pass the Great Arch of Zion, the largest of many blind arches in the park. The arch began forming through the action of groundwater seeping from a horizontal "spring line" in the canyon wall. Gravity and spalling of rock play an equal part in the enlargement, and eventual disappearance, of the arches. This photo shows the road under construction.

*T*his viewpoint at the west portal of the 1.1-mile-long tunnel is 800 feet above the canyon floor. The first of six tight switchbacks on this steep four-mile section of road is encountered here.

*D*edicated on July 4, 1930, the tunnel provided access to the slickrock section of the park and shortened the distance to Bryce and Grand Canyons. Several galleries provided excellent views of Zion Canyon for many years, but stopping in the tunnel is no longer permitted due to an increase in travel and safety considerations.

64

A 1930-vintage automobile exits the east end of the tunnel onto a high bridge spanning the upper reaches of Pine Creek.

*T*his view from on top of the Great Arch of Zion, with the West Temple as a backdrop for the switchbacks, is the reward for a half-mile hike (climb?) on the Canyon Overlook Trail from the steps at the east end of the tunnel.

*T*om Allen, park super-intendent in 1931, stands at the other tunnel on the East Side, which most local residents call The Little Tunnel. It was several years before the road got an asphalt surface.

*H*oodoos, stone columns on which a cap of iron con-cretions shields soft sandstone below from erosion, are common East Side features.

66

*C*heckerboard Mesa is the most prominent feature to greet park visitors inside the East Entrance. The checkerboarding phenomenon results from vertical weather cracks and horizontal bedding planes, and generally occurs on north-facing slopes.

*M*any of Zion's waterways follow fractures in the rock and develop narrow canyons. Here, though, rainwater and snowmelt find their own path of least resistance toward the Virgin River, lending shape and variety to the slickrock areas of the East Side.

The Human Impact

The first Mormon settlers in Zion Canyon described the Virgin River as a clear stream one could pole-vault from one grassy bank to the other. They also complained that they had to clear away tangles of wild roses in the valley in order to plant their crops.

The river was a capacious channel for run-off. In 1862, it rained steadily for two weeks or more before the river swelled to dangerous flood stage. Thirty years later, though, it seemed that every little shower brought a flood, and the people wondered where their farms—and homes—were going. Several communities were abandoned, and many of the canyon settlers moved elsewhere.

Did clearing and use of the land contribute to the ravaging floods? Certainly there were floods and there was erosion before there were people to use the land. Didn't Zion Canyon come about by erosion thousands of years ago?

Although those who lived within Zion Canyon utilized the land to capacity, it is ironic that most of the destructive floods originated outside the area of their influence. Many enormous herds of sheep devoured the vegetative cover of the watersheds of both

68

lthough a summer shower could spell trouble for settlers along the rampaging Virgin River, there was also beauty. More than one hundred waterfalls have been counted in the canyon during a single rainstorm. This 900-foot cataract at the Temple of Sinawava is a visitors' favorite. Similar falls help form "hanging canyons."

branches of the Virgin River. Without exception, these herds were owned by residents of surrounding counties.

The canyon settlers had taken possession of the land in and around the canyon some ten years before Major John Wesley Powell, an astute scientist as well as a bold explorer, came west and warned the nation about the delicate nature of all this western land and its limited resources. But who could have heeded his report, if they had read it?

Great numbers of cottonwoods that originally grew along the river had to be cut down for the building of homes, corrals and fences. There weren't sufficient stands of other trees accessible. The cottonwoods were usually cut in the fall or winter, too, so horses could eat the bark during the lean winter months. The less abundant native ash is a hardwood, and was needed for the building of strong wagons and farm tools.

Technology such as David Flanigan's cable and improved means of transportation eventually provided new sources to meet the canyon residents' needs, just as they led to the canyon becoming popular enough to be made a national park. The willingness of those first settlers—and their descendants, even today—to make certain sacrifices in order to bring about the reality of Zion National Park is commendable and has paid dividends in an improved local economy as well as preserving the natural wonders for all to see throughout the ages.

Summer showers meant torrents of muddy water from all the river's tributaries.

𝒜ll of the pioneers who settled near the present site of Zion Lodge moved out after about ten years of contention with the land-hungry river.

$\mathscr{T}$his view of the West Temple and Mount Kinesava
reveals a broad Virgin River floodplain nearly devoid of
vegetation.

72

*P*ark Service workers began early to retard the river's erosive action by building "hog-pens", log enclosures filled with rocks that jutted into the current to slow or redirect it.

*E*xtensive cribbing was necessary to protect the park roads and other structures from the flooding Virgin River. Various combinations of logs, boulders, net wire and cobblestone were used in experiments with riverbank stabilization.

$\mathcal{W}$hile the early experiments helped tame the river, river-bank stabilization techniques had reached a higher degree of sophistication by the time the Civilian Conservation Corps did this work in the mid-1930s.

*C*ontrol of the river (which included cooperative range management throughout the watershed) has helped the Fremont cottonwood reestablish itself in the riparian plant community, which is second only to the pinyon-juniper community in the park's higher elevations. The cottonwood is the largest and most abundant of the riverbank varieties.

*D*esert swamps thrive in oxbows, which are old meanders of the river bypassed by a controlled stream channel.

In Retrospect

*I*magine that Nephi Johnson returned one hundred years after his first visit and viewed the canyon from Observation Point. Except for a road and a few buildings, the scene may not have appeared to have changed much from this vantage point. Johnson had not witnessed the denudation and eventual restoration.

Upon closer inspection some changes would have been evident. The exotic tamarisk had replaced the sandbar willow and wild rose as the dominant undercover. Other introduced plants such as Russian thistle, puncture vine and purple mustard (*Chorispora tenella*) took over the disturbed areas. Also the desirable Indian ricegrass and wheatgrass had been almost crowded out by foxtail and cheatgrass.

Johnson would have found an increase in the deer and rodent populations due to the reduced number of predators, including the complete disappearance of grizzly bears and wolves. He would also have found beavers in the canyon—something he didn't mention on his 1858 trip. A letter written by one of the early settlers mentioned beavers and otters, but both have been absent through most of Zion's period of occupation. The otter has never returned. Maybe it will some day.

After Frederick Dellenbaugh first glimpsed Zion in 1872, he wrote ". . . few outlooks in all the world are superior for colour and form. . . ." His view was north from the Hurricane Ledge, toward Mount Kinesava.

Nephi Johnson came to Zion Canyon looking for home sites. Certainly your reason for coming was entirely different from his, as your lasting impression of the place will be. Should each visitor answer the question as to what impressed him or her most about Zion, the answers would probably be as numerous and varied as the visitors themselves. Some would marvel over this "Yosemite in Technicolor," where oxides of iron provide most of the color in the sandstone. Others would remember searching for the pinhead-sized Zion snail *(Physa zionis)*, one animal truly endemic to Zion. Listening to a naturalist relate the story of Nephi Johnson or some other phase of Zion's human history, while interesting, would not be rated as the outstanding experience. Your Zion experience will depend on many things, but most of all your interests and curiosity.

*T*he canyon itself has features that make it unique among the many colorful canyons of the western United States. The vertical walls and nearly flat bottom suggest glacial origin, yet Zion was formed by a stream. It is a contradiction to the rule that canyons formed by glaciers are U-shaped while those cut by streams are V-shaped. Here the Navajo Sandstone formation reaches its maximum thickness where vertical walls 2,000 feet high are common.

Water seeps to the surface at the base of the Navajo Formation, which is an excellent aquifer. The moisture forms a horizontal "spring line" throughout most of the canyon, and gives life to the "hanging gardens" which may be seen at Weeping Rock and along the Gateway to The Narrows Trail. (This is where the Zion snail is found.) The seepage also begins the formation of arches by dissolving the cementing material in the rock. In effect, this is erosion from the bottom upward, which keeps the canyon walls vertical.

*M*any visitors count the sacred datura, *Datura mete-loides*, as Zion's most representative plant. It is also called moon lily, since it blooms at night. Sitting in a patch of it isn't recommended. If you handle the plant, don't rub your eyes, as it may cause dilation of the pupils. Ingesting it could be fatal.

*Z*ion's memorable animals include the little canyon tree-frog. *Hyla arenicolor* isn't a true frog and is usually found on rocks instead of in trees. But it sometimes scares visitors with its mating call, which sounds very much like that of a male goat or sheep. Listen for it in spring-fed grottos during Spring and early Summer.

80

*B*lossoms and frog-songs, of course, are among the merely ephemeral beauties of Zion. Still, they are a part of the canyon's constant novelty, the kind that attracts thousands of visitors—and each of you, I hope—to return time and again. On each journey, you will be able to see the might and majesty of the canyon, from beside the river or from high on the rim, like old-timer wrangler Walt Beatty shown here at Observation Point. These colored cliffs will always be the basis for Zion Canyon's history; the rock, the flora and fauna, the people and the park endure.

The Ghosts of Zion

My childhood haunts keep beckoning to me.
Those playgrounds of my youth I long to see;
   But the routine of my day bids fancy wait
Until the canyon's call shall find me free.

Today I heard the call and came at last.
The spell of sweet nostalgia held me fast,
   And, giving in to pleasant reverie,
I mingled with the ghosts of Zion past.

In a grotto where I'd often been before,
I sat and dreamed, and let my spirit soar
   To bygone days and other scenes I knew,
As through a gossamer veil I shared the canyon's lore.

There was Nephi Johnson and his Paiute guide,
Who stayed at Oak Creek and refused to ride
   Into the place where the feared Wainopits dwells,
And would wait there only until eventide.

There appeared the image of one I didn't know,
Who stood awhile to watch the passing show.
   Then I recognized the ghost of Joseph Black,
When he winked at me and said, "I told you so.

"And I told my friends that someday they'd be sorry,
When the world would come and listen to my story.
   They laughed at me and said that I was daft,
And called my beautiful canyon 'Joseph's Glory'."

Near a place where Mount Majestic stands,
I saw Behunin, Heap and Rolf plow the river sands,

And Isaac name his haven "Little Zion"
With temples built by God and not by hands.

I wondered why those stalwarts moved away,
While many other builders came to stay.
   But, here or there, they left their marks in passing,
And I felt their spirits' presence here today.

In my mind's eye there was one familiar scene
Of sweating men—determined, bronzed and lean—
   Who built houses, roads, diversion dams and ditches,
As through their toil they made the valley green.

Then came the United States Geological Survey,
Whose photographers, artists and writers would convey
   To all mankind the beauty of this place.
Then it was plain the world was here to stay.

Next, men of foresight came and made a park
Of nature's gem; where soon I would embark
   Upon my life's career, and get my start
Where many men in green have left their mark.

I saw many superintendents come and go,
And greeted everyone I chanced to know;

Also my many pals at Zion Lodge—
Those friendships that I made I won't outgrow.

I shook hands with a President and movie star.
Crown Prince of Sweden came in chauffeured car.
    All this I hope to someday see again,
As I leave the doorway to my past ajar.

I thought to take my leave as day was done;
To come again and see if I had won
    A favored place; but paused again to see
A golden glow cast by a setting sun.

I turned and said, "Greetings, old Flanigan Peak."
A voice came back, "Take care to whom you speak,
    Brash upstart; you will not find here
The gift of immortality you seek.

"In tales you tell and pictures that you paint,
Your forebears oft appear without a taint;
    But while you venerate ancestral lore,
Antiquity alone does not make one a saint.

"Those ghosts of yesterday with whom you talk
Are merely squatters in this land, and mock
    The sanctity of these enduring shrines,
For flesh is not as durable as rock.

"Frail man, look quickly at my alpenglow;
For you shall pass, much as the winter snow.
    Long after you have gone I'll keep my watch.
I saw the Anasazi come and go."

"Great Watchman, I look up to you," I said,
"But let me also love my kindred dead,
    And all whose sweat and toil built thoroughfares
On which the feet of all the world now tread.

"I'll worship at these temples, not built by man,
And sing about their splendor while I can.
    But I would give the pioneer his due."
And the mountain smiled approval of my plan.

Then as I left I thought about my day,
And all my friends of now and yesterday.
    I know their deeds are graven in the stone,
Instead of lightly scribbled in the clay.

As long as I can feel and hear and see
I'll come here oft. Just save a nook for me.
    And when these senses dim, I'll take my place
Among the ghosts of Zion yet to be.

—J. L CRAWFORD

J. L. Crawford

84

Index